# WHERE A CAT BELONGS

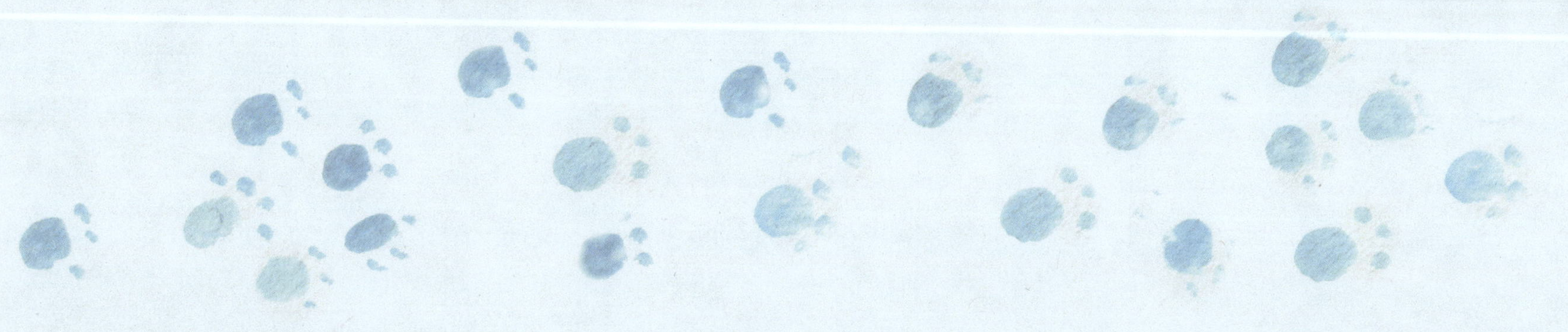

*In Ukrainian, there is a saying that to experience the world in someone else's shoes is to live "in their fur". We hope this book will lead you through some of Murzyk's adventures and that you will be able to experience his ups and downs—in his fur.*

*A special dedication to the Ukrainian families left behind and to those adjusting to their new lives abroad.*

First published in 2024

www.themurzykcat.com

Instagram – @theMurzykcat

ISBN: 979-8-9896177-1-5
Text copyright © Jacob Bourgeois and Polina Golubkova, 2024
Illustrations copyright © Bogdana Bondar, 2024
Consultant Editor – Leila Boukarim
Designer – Tubik Studio
Text Designer – Miruna Pria



9 8 7 6 5 4 3 2 1

Printed in the United States of America

This story is based on true events.

Jacob Bourgeois & Polina Golubkova

# Where a Cat Belongs

## Murzyk's Journey from Texas to Ukraine

My name is Murzyk. I was born on the dusty streets of San Antonio, Texas to a tough but loving cat mother. San Antonio can be a rough place to grow up. *"It's a cat-eat-cat city,"* she always told me. *"Remember to be strong and stand up for those you love, because I won't always be there to protect you."*

She was right. Kittenhood is short in San Antonio. I wish I could have followed her advice and stayed strong, but I didn't get along with the other cats. I always ended up in fights I couldn't win. I wasn't cut out for life on the streets. I'm more of a pussy cat than a panther, though sometimes I wish I were a panther.

1-10
410

My street life was cut short when one day I followed the tasty scent of tuna and found myself trapped in a cage. *The oldest human trick in the book!* I thought, as I stress licked.

I was poked all over, then corralled into a room full of other confused animals. Many humans came and went who wanted to hold me, but I was scared and preferred to stay in my cage. Something didn't feel right. *Where do I belong?* I wondered.

Finally, two humans entered. I felt their kindness right away. *"We want a special cat,"* one said. *"a cat who is loving but is having trouble finding a new home."*

This was my chance, and I knew what I had to do. I rubbed my strongest rub and purred my strongest purr. My mother raised me with good Texas manners after all.

*"What a beautiful cat you are! I'm going to give you a good Ukrainian name,"* my human mother said. *"My little Murzyk."*

*"Welcome home, Murzyk!"* What music to my furry ears! I'd never received so much love, so much cat-tention, and so many good scratches.

I finally had a family again, and there was nothing I wouldn't do for them. Except let them hold my paw—I'm paw-stingy. I just needed a little more time.

I was settling into the life of a house cat when everything changed again. *"We're moving to a city called Kyiv in Ukraine, Murzyk, where my family is from."*

I didn't know where or what a Kyiv was, but with my cat passport in paw, I did my best to take my cat mother's advice and put on a brave snout for my new family.

Our journey began. I gazed at the
changing landscapes as we sped
forward like a herd of wild horses.
I'd never been  outside of Texas
before—what a big world!

We made stops along the way for breaks.
I sniffed the air to discover the new smells
and rolled in the soft green grass.

Soon we were soaring through the clouds. I might have released my inner scaredy cat a bit, but I think I held it together pretty well.

*"We made it to Kyiv, Murzyk,"* my family reassured me, *"And it looks like there are many other animals who want to enter Ukraine."*

We waited in a long line full of yips, meows and whines. Finally, I had a chance to display my cat passport to a human with kind eyes. *"Welcome home, little cat,"* he said.

My family was busy unpacking, but
I was more concerned with discovering
new smells, scratching new pillows, and
suffering from serious catlag.

Kyiv felt so different from San Antonio. From my window, I watched Ukrainian cats playing and greeting passersby. *Is it difficult to be a streetcat in Kyiv?* I wondered.

With time, the skies grew darker, the trees went to sleep, and cotton fell from the sky. It was cold! But Ukrainians took good care of their street cats, delivering home cooked meals every day.

*"Let's show this Texas cat some snow."* My father smiled and carried me gently outside. *Finally, a chance to prove myself as a street cat in a new city,* I thought with all the cat confidence I could muster.

On second thought, I preferred the indoors. Once a house cat, always a house cat.

I truly felt I knew where I belonged, and it filled my little heart with joy. But all at once, something was different. My family spoke in hushed tones and there were tears in their eyes. In a moment, all of my pillows and toys were packed away into boxes left standing in the hallway.

Outside our window, I watched worried humans form lines at stores and stand under shelters with their pets. A thunderous sound ripped through the sky sending rumbles beneath my paws. *What is going on?* I wondered. *And why is everyone so scared?*

We left our home once again. But there were no smiles this time, no excitement, and no joy in my family's eyes. I wanted to help my family feel better. I think they really needed me in those moments.

We arrived in a safe place filled with many other people. Voices were faint, and everyone was tired. I decided it was time to put aside my fears and be the strong cat I knew I could be. I rubbed. I purred. I nuzzled. Eventually, I helped everyone smile again.

The cotton slowly disappeared, the storks made their nests, and the river returned to life, but we still didn't go home. *When will we go back?*

*"We need to leave Ukraine until our home becomes safe, Murzyk,"* my family said as they filled boxes with our belongings once again. I remembered our journey from San Antonio.

MURZYK

We drove past many fields and many towns. I never knew that Ukraine was so big—almost as big as Texas. Through the window, I noticed other pets like me with their families. *I wonder where they're going,* I thought. *Are they leaving Ukraine too?*

Our long journey ended in a city called Munich. I was tired, but happy to be somewhere where I could stretch my paws and feel the sun on my fur, with my family by my side. Finally, we had a place where we could rest.

I watched the seasons change from my new window. The animals on the streets reminded me of Ukraine. And of course, I carried out my cat duties and stayed strong for my family. As always, they needed me.

The life of a journeying cat is not always easy, and I will be happy to go back to Kyiv when we can. But as long as I have my family with me, I know that I will always be where I belong.